A DOG is a GIFT

A poetic celebration of living with a dog

Ken Nye

To the Mortons—

Ken Nye

Freeport, Maine

2008

Published by TJMF Publishing

Library of Congress Control Number: 2008909466
ISBN: 13 digit: 978-0-9801003-3-4   10 digit: 09801003-3-X

Copyright © 2008 by TJMF Publishing

Poems in this book are the property of Kenneth P. Nye
knye@maine.edu

All rights reserved
Printed in the United States of America
by Fidlar Doubleday of Michigan
October, 2008

Back cover photos by Paul Schreiber, of Yarmouth, Maine.

Front cover photo by Ken Nye, taken in 1978:
Tessy in Grampa's garden.

"Where's the puppy?" Entire family panicked,
searched the house and the fields for "the puppy."
I found her sitting serenely in Grampa's garden
amidst the hosta.

This book is dedicated to the dogs that have filled my life, from boyhood to the present, with companionship and affection and laughter. To:

• **BONNIE**, a black cocker spaniel, the dog of my childhood. She joined our family when I was two. She died when I was 18. I wasn't with her when she was put down. I should have been.

• **TAFFY**, a lab-collie mix, Ann's and my first family dog, the best Frisbee player I have ever known. She loved to get in under the covers with me when Ann wasn't looking.

• **MISSY**, our step-dog, a gentle and loveable golden retriever who celebrated my return to the house in the afternoon by presenting me with a stone dug up from the driveway. (In the thirteen years we lived on the farm, Missy moved our entire driveway ten feet.)

• **TESSY**, our first golden puppy, my farm and woods wandering companion, the first dog I trained, a special dog to me.

• **GRACIE**, a tiny blond cocker spaniel waif, rebuffed by her mom and rescued by my sister who fed her day and night for weeks with an eye dropper and spoon to keep her alive, blind in one eye, always grateful for our attention.

• **ROSIE**, a spunky blond cocker spaniel who, when we got a golden puppy (Barney), enjoyed bossing him around because she was bigger than he was, but who, when he had grown to be four times her size, could never figure out why he didn't do what she wanted him to.

• **BARNEY**, a great big golden, the only male dog I have ever raised, with a heart as big as his head and a love of people that knew no limits. He was a joy. I still miss him.

• **ELLIE AND FRANKIE**, our two abandoned golden retriever/ yellow lab mixed breeds who rescued me from grief, and who reminded me every day of the joy and affection that dogs bring into our lives.

• **COZY**, our new baby golden retriever (now two years old) who is everything a dog person could ask for in a dog: a sweet, obedient, snugglebunny who delights in chewing on Frankie's collar and neck, probably the last puppy I will ever have.

A Dog is a Gift reminds us of what is marvelous, magical, humorous, and profoundly moving about our relationships with our beloved canine companions. As Ken says so simply, his dogs "put a smile on living." But this little gem of a book is not just for dog lovers. for it will warm the heart of anyone who appreciates sweet memories of simple pleasures, and the joys we hold within. Ken touches those memories and those joys in these heartfelt poems about his dogs . . . "But they come to me if I call them. / So do all my dogs, those here and those gone. / They come to me if I call them."

Rebecca Pride, lifelong lover of dogs

TABLE OF CONTENTS

Foreword	7
What Is It About a Dog?	11
The Smell of a Dog	12
What Dogs Do	13
Walking the Dogs	15
Not Good News	18
"Let's Go for a Ride"	20
Reminders of a Dog Now Gone	22
Golden Retriever Rescue	23
I Never Met a Puppy I Didn't Like	24
Memories That Last a Lifetime	25
The Promise	29

FOREWORD

I am what some people refer to as a "dog person." I suppose that could mean all kinds of things. Boiled down to its essence, though, it simply means I love dogs. I always have. When I was a boy I slept with dogs, didn't mind, even was comforted by, their smell, delighted in the raspy love swipes of their tongues, usually understood pretty much what they were thinking, basked in their unbridled and obvious perception of me as a superior and loveable being.

I read somewhere that sociologists or anthropologists or people who study human cultures have determined that the dogs we live with and treat like members of the family did not come from a wild dog that was captured and brow beaten into submission and domesticity. They come from a strain of what originally was a wild dog but which, over eons of time, mutated into an animal that not only allowed itself to be taken into a human culture, actually relished that role. We do not live with wolves, who, even in captivity and treated with kindness, maintain their wild demeanor and for whom living with humans is exactly that – "captivity." We live with animals who would rather sleep next to us than next to other dogs.

When I was a boy, I read every dog story I could get my hands on. I can remember reading *The Call of the Wild* when I was about 15 and wiping the tears from my eyes as I read the story of Buck being asked by his beloved master to break the half-ton snow sled out of the ice and tow it a hundred yards. I can still see the man who had wagered his entire personal wealth on this challenge leaning down to talk into Buck's ear, imploring him, "As you love me, Buck. As you love me;" and then hearing the crowd of gold miners and bar maids cheering uncontrollably as Buck lunged back and forth, first breaking the runners free and then increasing speed as he strove toward the 100 yard marker for the human being he loved and who loved him. I could barely see the words on the last pages of *Where the Red Fern Grows* and *The Incredible Journey,* my eyes were so full of tears.

The dogs in my life have been loving companions who, for the most part, tried to do what I wanted them to do. But, like all children, they sometimes misbehaved, got carried away in their cantankerousness and were a pain in the neck. But that is all part of the package you get with a dog. Too many people fall in love with an adorable puppy, ignoring or not cognizant of the reality that eventually the cute little puppy is going to become a teenager and then a young adult who isn't so cute anymore, and they discard the dog, throwing not only the dog out of their lives but an opportunity to experience limitless devotion and unconditional love.

In the poems in this little book, I try to focus not only on the magical difference in human lives that a relationship with a dog can bring, but on the inevitable end of those relationships. James Herriott talks in the introduction to one of his books about the deal we make when we adopt a puppy. On that first ride home with the puppy in the back seat, the car full of laughs and joy and giggles, we bring home a new family member who will grow into the hearts of the people he will love and to whom he will become devoted. But, Herriott points out, the price we pay for that love and devotion is the last trip to the vet's where, out of love, we say goodbye. We have all made this trip. But that doesn't render it easier for the heart to absorb. I have left the vet's office more than once unable to talk, barely able to see through the tears.

There are moments of sadness and loss in these pages. But, I hope you will recognize as well the joy in these poems that matches the joy in your own heart when you remember and reflect on the wondrous gift that is a dog.

KEN NYE
Autumn, 2008

POEMS

WHAT IS IT ABOUT A DOG?

What is it about a dog,
these almost-half-human animals
who choose us over
their own kind?
Is it the look in the eyes?
The silent pledge of loyalty
and holy commitment?

Is it the shy but determined approach toward
the hand of a stranger, held out for inspection and approval,
the obvious desire to please?
Is it the joyful ecstasy that pours from
the face,
the happy canine grin,
the wild exuberance of a tail out of control
when the master returns or
the leash is pulled from the closet?

Was there ever a creature more forgiving,
willing to accept responsibility
for whatever is wrong in your life
that prompted that unfair
reproof and harsh word of rejection?

Does anyone else read your body language
as accurately?
Are the heavy thoughts in your head
as apparent to anyone else
as they are to your dog,
who always knows what you are feeling
and who always offers support
with a nudge of the arm
or a wet love swipe with the tongue?

What do you suppose happened in God's world
that gave him the idea to create a dog?

Loyal friend, loving companion,
ever present attendant who offers
love without boundaries,
devotion without reason.

A dog is a gift.

THE SMELL OF A DOG

Ever since I was a boy,
I have loved the smell of a dog's paws —
leathery pads, edged with fur
that absorb the rich, musty fragrances
of where the dog and I have been
in our adventures together.

I love the smell of the top of a dog's head,
where the fur is usually cleaner than any other
part of the animal.
The top-of-the-head smell is fresher than the paw,
more like the smell of a little boy's hair
at the end of a summer's day in the sun.

I don't mind
the faint smell of skunk on a dog,
(but only if it's faint).
Snuggling down for a nap
with my skunk-flavored companion
lying next to me
puts me back in another time,
when the world was new,
waiting to be explored and discovered
by my friends and me and our dogs;
when the little lame balloon man
was simply another reason to wonder.

WHAT DOGS DO

Most dogs do not herd sheep,
search for skiers caught in avalanches,
chase escaped convicts with their noses.
What most dogs do most of the time is sleep.
And if they aren't sleeping, they sit around
hoping someone will drop some food on the floor.
Dogs sleep so much, a person might think
that is really all they do.

But, as I sit here and look at my two pals sitting at my feet,
I can think of lots of other things that dogs do, too.
They earn their keep.

They love unconditionally.
And they are totally non-discriminatory
about whom they love.
They don't care what color you are,
what language you speak,
whether you sometimes wear a skirt or not,
with whom you sleep,
how much you weigh,
or for whom you voted.
Even if you're not a very nice person,
your dog will think you are.

Dogs are multi-lingual.
Introduce your dog to a person from Estonia,
and the two will immediately have a conversation.

Dogs have E.S.P.
They know whether or not
you're feeling good about yourself
before you do.

Dogs are totally uninhibited,
not caring if they look foolish
when the kids dress them up in doll clothes,
or when they moan in ecstasy
when you rub their stomachs.

Dogs live in the moment.
They don't' wonder what will happen tomorrow
because they have no understanding of tomorrow.
When they awake it's a brand new day in which to
eat, sleep, explore, and eat again.

And no matter what the mirror tells us in the morning,
the message when we get to the kitchen is,
"Oh, wonderful person, you look so beautiful, poised
and charming this morning.
I am overjoyed to see you again.
I can't wait until we do something together today.
But I know you have a busy schedule,
and so I will wait here on my bed until you need me.
As you know, I love you dearly and think you are the sun."

What more could a person want in a companion?

No wonder our dogs live in our hearts, even when they are gone.

WALKING THE DOGS

In retirement
I have become a volunteer walker of the dogs
at the local shelter.
I have learned that when I open the door
to the kennels in the back of the building,
there will be instant bedlam.

It appears that the dog in the pen nearest the door
has been assigned the task by the rest of the inmates
to let them know
when someone other than staff comes in,
and he takes his job very seriously.
Even though I've been there a number of times already,
he doesn't consider me staff.
(Anybody who is not staff is considered "new.")

So I open the door
as quietly as I can.

He is dozing, but when he lifts an eyelid
to check the door, he sees me
trying to slip through,
and in an instant
he's up and announcing my arrival.
"Visitor! He's new! He's new! New visitor!"

House rules apparently call for 100%
participation in the welcome,
so they all celebrate my arrival
at a decibel level that suggests their goal
in this raucous welcome is to let the rest of the world
know that I have entered their kennel.

In an effort to quell the noise as fast as I can,
I kneel down in front of one of the cages
and begin to simply talk quietly to the soul
on the other side of the chain-link fencing.
In just a few seconds
the rest quiet down, resigned to the fact that they
are not the one the visitor chose.

Which dog I will leash and take out the door
is strictly a matter of my whimsy.
Sometimes I rise to the challenge of the loud pit
bull/Norwegian elkhound
who has never been leash trained and drags me through the
woods
like an ox twitching lumber to the wood yard.
And other times I feel an affinity for one of the little ones,
not as aggressive as the big dogs.

Today it's the beagle-pug
with the smushed-up nose and soulful gaze.
I enter the dog's pen, leash in hand,
and sit down,
extend my hand for the dog to sniff,
explaining that I have come to take her for a walk
on the woods trail.

At first she is a little aloof,
but when I sit down and extend my hand,
she warms up to me and comes over to be caressed.

These are all beautiful, affectionate animals.
How did they end up here?
(I myself have two golden-labs that were abandoned
by a family that moved out of town.
How those people could have driven
off leaving
that loveable pair
is beyond me.)

I attach the leash to the little beagle-pug's collar,
and we head out the back door.

She hasn't been leash trained either,
but she doesn't have the weight
to give me a hard time,
so we have a nice gentle stroll on the woods path.

We pass other dogs on the trail who ignore her
as rudely as she ignores them.
Neither of them is going to waste time
checking out the other one when there are
more important things to do ——
sniffing the urine messages left
on the legs of the resting benches,
looking into chipmunk holes,
drinking from the stream that flows under
the walk bridge.

Eventually we are back at the shelter.
(Coming into the kennel through the back door
does not create the excitement that an announced
new visitor would generate.)

I lead the little dog back to her kennel,
take the leash off, bend down and she gives me a kiss.
I tell her I hope she is not here the next time I come.

I hang up the leash
and tell the gang I'll see them all Thursday.
But none seems to be cheered by those words.
They want to go home with someone.

NOT GOOD NEWS

The vet called with the biopsy report.
It's not good.
The bad kind of cancer.
She said chemo therapy
could control it for a while,
long enough to give him another year or so.
But it's going to cost money.

There really isn't much to debate here.
How can we even consider not giving him
the possibility of that extra year?
Calling him a "family pet"
seems to put him into the same category
as a favorite easy chair, something you grow
comfortable with but when it's too old
and beat up to keep around
you drop it off at the Salvation Army
and go and get another one.

But the comfortable easy chair
doesn't love you unconditionally like
this old warrior who protects us from squirrels
and low flying planes,
who monitors our moods like a weather man and
moves in to just sit and offer support or
slip his nose under the hand
when he senses somebody is down.

The wonderful thing about this situation
(if there is anything good to be said about it)
is that he doesn't have a clue.
All he knows is that he's feeling good again.
He's not worrying about the cancer coming back
or about getting sick from the chemo.
He'll just take one day at a time,
relish the opportunities each day gives him
to play ball and eat great food,
("Where have they been keeping this stuff called
table scraps?")
ride in the back seat,

stick his head out the window
and let the wind blow his cheeks out.
It's a great life, and he has no worries about the future.
There is still a smile on his face.

Of course, we'll go with the chemo therapy.
We'll give him as much time as we are allowed.
We're probably going to spoil him rotten.

I'll call the vet

"LET'S GO FOR A RIDE"

I get the same response that I've always gotten:
a look of excitement and joy,
immediate effort to rise and head for the car.
But rising is now a major project,
and jumping up into the
back seat is not possible.
So I lift him up, moving mechanically,
trying to drive my grief and dread down into my gut.

How many times have I said, "Let's go for a ride"?
The sunroof was for him so he could stand
on the center console and poke his huge head up
through the roof and survey the passing world
like a tank commander.

I got a kick out of people smiling and pointing
when they saw him.
No smile for him, though.
Piloting this tank is serious business.

But no more tank commander trips now.
Legs are too wobbly.

He just lazes on the back seat,
enjoying being with me.
I talk to him and get the usual unspoken,
"I don't have any idea what you are talking about,
but I love you anyway" look.

White hair around the face now,
eyes glazed with age.
Even though he can barely see,
he'll go wherever I go.
That's been his life purpose.

My hands shake on the wheel
as I contemplate our farewell.

Only a little while back he was an armful of puppyness,
for years a constant companion and playmate,
always striving to do what I wanted him to do.
Snuggling down on my feet under the desk,
he wanted to be close.

So I owe him this last trip,
when he is still a dignified presence
in the backseat.

We'll park the car, I'll put the leash on him
and help him down.
And when he recognizes where we are,
he'll begin to shake like he always does.
But, like a trooper, he'll go wherever I go.

I will miss him so

REMINDERS OF A DOG NOW GONE

We no longer have dog-hair tumbleweeds
blowing along the surface of the hardwood floors or
lurking in corners and crevasses of wall and baseboard.
But occasionally, cleaning an out-of-the-way closet,
I come across another dainty phantom-like wisp
of golden retriever underdown that reminds me of him.

Waxing the bathroom floor,
I see the chewed edges of the baseboard
where he experimented with wood trim
as a way to pass the time until we got home.

Out in the garage, looking for the plumber's snake
with which to probe the septic line,
I confront at eye level his choke-chain collar
with the license tag
hanging from a nail in one of the ceiling joists.
It seems to be out of place, hanging from a nail.
It belongs around his neck.

I wonder what the point is now of a car with a sunroof.
No big golden retriever to stand on the center console
and make the world smile.

Rather than making me sad, though,
these unexpected encounters with a dog now gone
warm my mood,
soften any edges clinging to thoughts and attitudes
of the moment,
much in the same way he leveled my emotions
and put a smile on living.

He is still here and there,
still a presence in my heart.

GOLDEN RETRIEVER RESCUE

Our golden retriever died a few months ago.
He was eleven.
Our house was empty and my heart was hollow,
but I figured I'd wait until summer to get a puppy.

One empty day followed another.
There was no dog at my feet at the breakfast table,
no thumping tail drumming a welcome against the side of the
car
as I drove into the garage,
no pestering wet nose flipping my arm
off the computer keyboard to
remind me it's dinner time.

The world probably thought I was the same person,
but my wife knew something was missing.
She called the local Golden Retriever rescue network —-
found two golden retriever/ Lab "mixed breeds"
waiting for a home.
Raised together and
abandoned together,
the shelter wanted them to go out together.
We went up to "see if you like them."

My days now start with a group hug and
a lovingly administered face wash,
a new morning ritual that makes me wonder
who rescued whom.

I NEVER MET A PUPPY I DIDN'T LIKE

Once in a while, I see a dog
straining at his chain,
lips curled as he hurls oaths of hatred at me,
dragging his doghouse in an effort
to latch on to my leg or tear my face.

And I think to myself,
"Why in the world would anyone want a dog like that?"

Then I wonder if that dog came out of the litter box
as an eight-week-old puppy
angry and full of fury.

Can there be such a thing as a "vicious puppy"?

I have never seen one.

As a boy
I worked at a private kennel
owned by millionaires,
a hunting family who raised Cocker and English spaniels
for companionship and field work.
I cleaned out pens,
took young adult dogs for walks in the fields,
preparing them for full-time training on leash and off.

The highlight of my day was my half-hour lunch break,
when, after inhaling a tuna fish sandwich,
I'd go into the puppy pen and sit against the wall.
Fifteen to thirty puppies, squealing in delight,
swarmed over me, onto my lap, climbing my chest
to give me kisses.
A joy-filled thirty minute love fest.
I never saw a bad puppy,
never experienced a puppy bite offered as anything other
than a love bite.

"Vicious puppy"?

I don't think so.

MEMORIES THAT LAST A LIFETIME

I.
I was sitting at the dinner table
when I was about ten,
having been told I was staying there until
the casserole on my plate was gone.
Everyone else had left the table
except Bonny, sitting silently at my feet,
hidden by an oversized table cloth.
She and I sat there for about fifteen minutes
as the casserole slowly disappeared.
It was a sticky business.
(I think my mother knew what we were up to,
but she was tired of the hassle
to get me to eat the casserole,
so she played dumb.)

II.
Taffy, Ann's and my first family dog,
never learned how to swim
because she hated being in any water
in which she couldn't touch bottom.
But when we spent time at the lake,
she loved to go out in the boat with me.

When she and I were out fishing one day,
I caught a perch too small to keep,
so I threw it back into the lake.
A sea gull saw me throw the fish,
and came soaring over, hoping the fish
might still be close to the surface.
Tafffy had always enjoyed chasing the sea gulls off our beach,
but the brazenness of this gull offended her.
Standing on the middle seat of the boat,
she started barking furiously
up at the sea gull, and as it glided over us
from one side of the boat to the other,
Taffy went with it.
Still barking up at the sea gull,
she walked right off the boat into the lake
and sank like a rock.

(It was amazing how instantaneously
the loud barking stopped.)
After a few seconds she came to the surface,
plunging her front legs into the water
trying to stay afloat,
wide eyed with fright.
I grabbed her by the collar and hoisted her back into the boat.
But I must admit that I was laughing so hard,
I could barely see.

III.
Barney, our big male golden who loved the world
and everyone in it,
considered himself the pre-wash cycle
of our after-dinner clean-up.
He would stand next to the open dish washer
getting anything we'd missed.
One evening, I was rinsing and loading dishes
and Barney was pre-washing.
As he leaned in to get a tiny morsel left on a plate,
his collar caught one of the tines of the rack.
And as he backed out, the rack moved with him.
Thinking he had been grabbed by the attacking dishwasher
he broke for the far side of the kitchen,
filling the air with dishes, cups. glasses and silverware
from the rack still attached to his collar.
The whole thing took place in only seconds,
ending with Barney huddled
under the hanging jackets,
with the dish rack on his head,
looking pathetic.
But it was funny.

IV.
These three characters are gone now.
So, too, are Missy, Tessy, Gracie, Rosie and Ellie.
But I have them right here, inside of me.
They are part of me now.

Frankie and Cozy, my two companions
lying on the floor next to me,
will go outside in a minute to go woodsing
or to hang out down by the road,
hoping walkers will come by whom they can greet.

But they come to me if I call them.
So do all my dogs, those here and those gone.
They come to me if I call them.

THE PROMISE

I lie back in the chair
and place the puppy
that smells of warm milk
on my chest.
She crawls up under my chin
and tries to suckle.
Getting no results,
she snuggles down to sleep
on my neck,
breathing contentment into my ear,
whispering her promise of life-long devotion.

ACKNOWLEDGEMENTS

My thanks to Scott Vile, of the Ascensius Press in South Freeport, Maine, for his patience and skill in designing and formatting this book (and my other two books as well). Scott's expertise has given my books a touch of class which I never would have been able to do by myself.

My thanks and admiration to Paul Schreiber, of Yarmouth, Maine, for his patience and skill as a photographer. He took many, many wonderful pictures that did not end up in this book, but they will, sometime, somewhere, be seen by the public. They are terrific.

And I am indebted to Wanda Whitten, a talented, honest, tactful editor of my poems since shortly after I began writing, who spent hours reading and critiquing my poems.

And I am always appreciative of the up-beat attitude and help of my publisher, Jim Furber, who handles the nitty-gritty production/printing process, ensuring that it is of high quality and fairly priced.

And, lastly, most of my books would still be in the boxes in which they were shipped if it weren't for the unending initiative, energy, and enthusiasm of my sales manager Holly Eddy. The reason *Searching for the Spring* is in its seventh printing and *From the Heart* is in its third printing is Holly.

A book, especially one written by someone who is not experienced in the field of publishing, is the product of a team of people. I have been lucky that my team is so good.

Ken Nye
October, 2008

ABOUT THE AUTHOR

KEN NYE is a relatively new voice in Maine poetry, having begun his career as a poet only four years ago at the age of 62. After 42 years in public education as a high school English teacher, high school principal and college professor, Ken discovered the magic of poetry and began using it to reflect upon his life in all of its dimensions. He is a lover of the woods and waters of Maine, is surrounded by family and friends (his daughter and two granddaughters live right across the street, and his son and a granddaughter and grandson are an hour away) and is a life-long lover of dogs, all of which are the focus of his poetry.

Ken lives with his wife and soul-mate of 46 years, Ann, in Freeport. Counting the Nye's two dogs and the Nye's granddogs, there are six dogs in the Nye house at Thanksgiving and Christmas.